LifeTimes

The Story of
Martin Luther King

by James Riordan
illustrated by Rob McCaig

Belitha Press

First published in the UK in 2001 by
Belitha Press Ltd
London House, Great London Wharf
Parkgate Road, London SW11 4NQ

Produced for Belitha Press by
White-Thomson Publishing Ltd
2/3 St Andrew's Place
Lewes, BN7 1UP

ISBN 1 84138 341 4

British Library Cataloguing in Publication Data for this
book is available from the British Library.

Editor: Steve White-Thomson
Designer: Simon Borrough
Language consultant: Norah Granger, Senior Lecturer
  in Primary Education at the University of Brighton.

With thanks to Kay Barnham for her editorial help
in the latter stages of this book.

Printed in China

This book is to be

Introduction

Martin Luther King Jr was born on 15 January 1929 in Atlanta, Georgia, USA. At the age of 19, Martin became a Baptist minister like his father and devoted the rest of his life to preaching God's word and helping the black community.

At that time, black people in the southern states had few rights. If they tried to protest, they risked being put in jail. Worse still, they might be burnt or lynched by white people.

In early December 1955, Martin had just become minister of the Dexter Baptist Church in Montgomery, Alabama...

The Seat on the Bus

Her name was Rosa Parks. She lived in
Montgomery, in the southern state of Alabama.
Her job in a store did not pay much and
Rosa worked long hours to make ends meet.

One evening after work, Rosa caught the
bus as usual. She had been on her feet all day,
and was exhausted.

It was rush hour and the bus was almost full.
All the back seats were taken, so Rosa had to
sit in the middle, behind the whites-only seats.

At the next stop, some white people got on. They sat at the front of the bus, but one man had to stand.

The driver looked back at Rosa.

'Give him your seat!' he shouted loudly. In this town it was the law that black people had to give up the middle seats of a bus to white people.

But today Rosa was tired. She didn't feel like giving up her seat.

'No, I won't,' she said calmly, before turning to stare out of the window.

'Hey, nigger woman!' cried the driver, getting angry. 'You heard me. Give the white man your seat!'

She sighed. Why should she stand for a man just because he was white?

'No, I won't!' Rosa repeated, louder this time.

Other passengers, white and black, glared
at her. She was holding up the whole bus.

'Stand or I'll call the cops!' warned the driver.

But, for once, Rosa didn't care. Let the cops
come. She was sick of being pushed around.

Within a few minutes, two policemen had
arrived and she was on her way to jail.

Much later, Rosa was charged with breaking the city's bus laws.

'I understand,' she replied with a sigh. 'Now, I've waited a long time and it's hot. May I have a drink of water, please?' she asked.

'No, lady. Ours is a whites-only water tap.'

'But it isn't a whites-only phone,' she said.

'I can make one phone call.'
Rosa knew her rights.
After all, she'd worked
for the local Black Help
organization.
So she phoned a friend.
'Brother,' she said, 'I'm in
jail for sitting on a bus.'
Little did she know
what she was starting.

For 300 years, millions of black Africans had been taken to America as slaves. In 1865 slavery ended, yet several states in the south refused to give black people equal rights.

When Rosa Parks made her bus protest in 1955, she broke Alabama's segregation laws. The laws gave the best jobs, schools and restaurants to white people... and the best bus seats too.

The Boycott

The next day, Rosa met black church leaders at the Dexter Baptist Church. The minister was a young man called Martin Luther King.

There was silence when Rosa finished her story.

Then one man spoke. 'Law's law,' he said. 'You must obey the law.'

'Anyway, there's nothing we can do about it,' said another.

Suddenly, the young minister jumped up.
'Oh, yes there is!' he said. 'We'll all stay off
the buses. That way the bus company will lose
money. Then they'll have to treat us right.'

Not everyone agreed. Many were scared
of the white people.

'Oh yeah, and get ourselves burned alive!'

'Or our homes bombed.'

'What do you think, Rosa?' said the minister.

All eyes turned on her.

'I think it's time we stood up for our rights,' she said quietly.

'Or sit in your case,' someone said.

Everyone laughed. That broke the ice. It was agreed and the call went out to all black people – DON'T RIDE THE BUSES.

On Sunday night, the young minister walked slowly home. Martin was tired and worried.

Later, unable to sleep, he paced the floor, trying to comfort his two-week-old daughter. He thought about what he'd started.

What if it didn't work? Things would be worse than before – and white people would laugh at them.

The first bus of the day was due to pass his
house at 6 am. But he couldn't bear to watch.

Then, suddenly, his wife Coretta called out,
'Martin, Martin, come quickly!' He ran into
the front room just as the bus went by.

It was empty!

Fifteen minutes later the second bus was
empty too. And the third, and the fourth...

The early buses were usually packed
with black workers.

The boycott was working!

A year before Rosa Park's bus protest, the Supreme
Court had ruled that segregation in schools must end.
White and black children and students could go to the same
schools and colleges. The law also said that black people
could vote. But in the South nothing changed, and white
people stopped black people from voting. Most black
people were too afraid to demand their rights.

Love Your Enemy

That day Martin and Rosa drove round town.
It was unbelievable – the streets were packed.
   Men and women were walking as far as
ten kilometres to their downtown jobs.
Students were thumbing lifts to school.
And an entire family was riding a farm horse.

There wasn't a single black person waiting
for a bus. Young black people stood on street
corners, cheering and clapping the walkers
and horse riders.

Outside City Hall a jazz band was playing:
Ain't gonna ride them buses no more.
Ain't gonna ride them buses no more.
Why in hell don't the white folks know
I ain't gonna ride them buses no more.
The fight for black rights had begun.

That evening Rosa went with Martin to
a meeting. So many people turned up that the
speeches had to be broadcast to them outside.

When Martin spoke, he was very nervous,
looking round at Rosa for encouragement.

'We have to show white people we won't
be kicked about any more,' he said.
'We should follow Rosa's example:
protest with dignity. No violence.
And another thing: we shouldn't
hate our white brothers.'

Some people shook their heads.
A voice shouted, 'How can you
love someone who hates you?'

'It isn't easy,' Martin said.
'But we must always
remember Jesus' words:
"Love your enemy."
In any case, if it comes
to an open fight, the
white people would win.
They have the guns, the
tanks and the power.'

But not all white people were racists. Some, especially in the north, wanted justice for all.

'We will make such a fuss, peacefully,' said Martin finally, 'that the whole world will get to know about us.

Rosa sat listening to Martin speak. She had never heard anyone like him. He seemed to express everyone's thoughts so clearly, inspiring everyone. When he sat down, there was a hush.

Then all through the church and streets outside, people began to shout, clap and sing. They had found a leader.

While he was at college, Martin Luther King read about the life of Mahatma Gandhi. The Indian leader believed in non-violent protest and had led the people of India against British rule. He told his people they must be ready to go to jail, even die for freedom – but never kill for it.

Martin Luther King firmly believed that black people in the USA should follow Gandhi's ideas.

Montgomery Miracle

News of the 'Montgomery Miracle' spread across the country. Black people everywhere began to follow the Montgomery example, and a number of white people gave their support.

But other white people were angry. They thought the world was laughing at them. In desperation, they began a bombing campaign, even blowing up Martin's house. Luckily, the bomb went off on the porch. Baby Yoki was sleeping at the back of the house; Coretta was in the kitchen. They were unharmed.

This time Martin Luther King's family had escaped. But would he and his followers have the courage to fight on?

All over the south, black people guarded churches and houses, lighting them up at night.

One night, black people in Montgomery were woken by carloads of Ku Klux Klansmen rumbling through their district. The aim was clear: to scare black people into behaving 'like niggers should.'

But this time black people stood up to them. Inspired by Martin, they didn't hide indoors and turn out the lights. Not this time! They switched on all the lights, opened their doors and stood at the gates, waving and jeering.

The Ku Klux Klan were not used to being treated like a parade of circus clowns.

The black people appealed to the Supreme Court in faraway Washington to decide on their boycott of the buses.

To their surprise, the court said that bus segregation was against the law. Martin and his supporters had won!

The next day, Martin and Rosa got on a bus together.

The driver stopped Rosa. 'Are you the Mrs Parks who started the boycott?' he asked.

'Yes, I am.'

'Welcome aboard, lady,' he said with a smile. 'Take any seat and have a nice day.'

The three demands made by the bus boycotters were: that bus drivers should be polite to black people; that passengers should take their seats on a first-come, first-served basis; and that there should be black drivers on routes that black people used most.

Until these demands were met, the black people of Montgomery stayed off the buses.

Sit-ins

The Montgomery bus boycott was only the start. It inspired all sorts of protests throughout the south. One type of protest was the sit-in. One day Martin went into a fast-food store with Yoki, who was now five years old.

'Burger and fries, please,' he said politely. 'And a banana milkshake for my girl.'

People stared.

What was this black man doing in a whites-only restaurant? At first, the staff ignored him. Patiently, he kept repeating his order. Finally, the manager shouted, 'Look, boy, we don't serve niggers. So, git!'

Martin said nothing. He just sat down at a table with Yoki. More black people entered, asking to be served.

Every day they came back. Others did
the same in shops and libraries. No one
was served.

Stores began to lose money. The black
sit-ins scared white customers away. At the
end of the week, the manager of the fast-food
store came over to Martin.

'Here are your burger and fries, Sir,' he said.
'And a banana milkshake, miss. Thank you
for your custom.'

Slowly but surely, other shops and restaurants throughout the southern states did the same. And in the parks, black people sat themselves down on the whites-only benches. They came to realize an important truth: freedom is never given, it has to be won.

Not every campaign ended peacefully.
One evening, people were gathered in Martin's
church. All at once, bombs smashed through
the windows and a fire started. At first it
looked like they would all burn to death.
But firemen arrived just in time to save them.

Others were not so lucky. When a bomb
exploded in a Baptist church in Birmingham,
Alabama, four young girls died and 21 people
were badly hurt.

News of the actions by white mobs shocked the world.

One day, the phone rang in Martin Luther King's house.

'My name is John Kennedy,' a voice said. 'I'm running for President and I want to help you.'

The tide was turning. Things were starting to change.

After the 11 southern states lost the American Civil War in 1865, white racists set up the Ku Klux Klan. This terrible organization killed many hundreds of black people, usually by burning them alive or hanging (lynching) them from trees. Many Klan members held important jobs, even in the police and the Mayor's office.

We Shall Overcome

Though times were changing, there was
one town still ruled by fear and hatred
– Birmingham, Alabama. Here black people
lived in fear of their lives. Libraries had even
banned a book about black and white rabbits!

'If we can end segregation in Birmingham,'
Martin told his supporters, 'we can stop
it everywhere.'

He was up against tough opposition.

The State Governor George Wallace and the police chief 'Bull' Connor warned people, 'The streets will run with blood if dirty niggers cause trouble.'

It was Good Friday, a warm sunny day,
when Martin led a march down the main
street. A line of police blocked their path,
so the protesters linked hands, knelt and sang
hymns. The police rushed in with clubs and
police dogs, taking hundreds off to jail. It
looked like the end of the Birmingham protest.

What happened next made history.

If grown-ups were afraid, children were not.
From all over town a thousand black children,
some as young as six, came to join Martin.
They marched in twos, waving banners
and shouting, 'Freedom now!'

When Bull Connor saw them,
he screamed, 'Let those little niggers
have it! See those niggers run!'

People *did* see. Millions saw, all round the world. They watched the TV pictures with horror. Connor was laughing and police were hitting children to the ground. Police dogs were snarling and firemen were holding hoses. Children were crying and covered in blood.

So it went on, day after day. Then something odd happened. As usual, Connor ordered his men to attack. But this time, they didn't move.

'Damn it! Turn on the hoses!' he cried.

But, silently, the police and firemen turned aside – some had tears in their eyes. Martin's peaceful protest had won – thanks to the children.

Martin worked hard travelling up and down the country, telling the world about black people's problems. He went on some Freedom Rides when black people took buses from one state to another, sitting where they liked. That way, the protest movement spread. People began to realize that if they joined together to protest, they were strong.

The Freedom Rides, boycotts and sit-ins hit the white racists where it hurt most – it made them lose money.

Martin Escapes Death

By now Martin had become leader of the black civil rights movement. 'We're on the move,' he said. 'Like an idea whose time has come, not even mighty armies can stop us.'

While in jail Martin wrote his famous *Letter from a Birmingham Jail*. He was replying to an attack on him by eight white ministers. He explained what it was like to be black:

'When your last name is 'nigger', your middle name 'boy', your last name 'John', when you're never Mr or Mrs…'

The white ministers had told him to wait for rights to be given, to which he replied, '*Wait* nearly always means *never*.'

Being in the public eye, Martin received hundreds of letters every day. Many were from black people thanking him and saying, 'We are proud to have you as our leader.'

But he also got sackfuls of hate mail from white racists. There were some people who wanted him dead.

One day he was signing copies of his
book in New York when a woman came up.
'Are you Martin Luther King?' she asked.
'Why, yes, I am,' he replied with a smile.
At that, the woman thrust a knife into his
chest. He was rushed to hospital where the
knife was removed. It had just missed his heart.

Many times Martin went to jail, once for
four months' hard labour. The racists did all they
could to break him. But he battled on, believing
that, 'Freedom is never given to anybody.
It has to be forced from the authorities.'

During the summer of 1961, the Freedom Rides started
to end bus segregation between states as well as in
towns. The first freedom riders to reach Alabama were
beaten up by the Ku Klux Klan, who set fire to their bus.
People everywhere were shocked. The US Supreme Court was
forced to make segregation on buses between states illegal.

I Have a Dream

In the summer of 1963, Martin attended a civil rights rally at the Lincoln statue in Washington. As many as a quarter of a million people came from all over the country. There were poor black farm workers from the south. There were famous film stars, such as Marlon Brando and Sidney Poitier. There were as many white people as black people, with black and white children linking arms. It was the largest crowd in civil rights history.

Martin was the last speaker. He had spent hours planning his speech. Yet, as he gazed at the sea of faces, he threw aside his notes and spoke from the heart.

'I have a dream,' he cried, 'of an Alabama where little black boys and black girls will be able to join hands with little white boys and white girls as sisters and brothers.'

Swaying to and fro, people shouted, 'Dream some more!'

He dreamed that freedom and justice would one day come to all America; that one day everyone would come together and sing the old freedom song: *'Free at last, Free at last. Thank God Almighty, we're free at last!'*

Martin gave the most moving speech people had ever heard. As they listened, tears streamed down their cheeks. Could the dream really come true?

In the White House afterwards, President Kennedy shook Martin's hand and said, 'That's my dream, too. You know, Martin, millions of white people have heard your message for the first time. We must fight racism together.'

Martin added a word of warning.

'Remember, a hundred years ago, President Lincoln was shot for ending slavery.'

The two men shook hands warmly. Whatever happened to them, they knew that one day their dream would come true.

Three months later President Kennedy was shot dead while driving with his wife through Dallas, Texas. Five years after that, in 1968, Martin was shot dead too, on the balcony of his hotel room in Memphis, Tennessee. He was only 39. But his short life changed the lives of millions of black Americans.

On his gravestone are the words: 'Free at last. Free at last. Thank God Almighty, I'm free at last.'

The Civil Rights Movement

The Civil Rights Act of 1875 claimed to give black Americans the same rights as white Americans, although many years would go by before all citizens really *were* equal.

By 1900, 18 states in north and west America had decided on various ways of tackling racial discrimination. Meanwhile, states in southern America supported segregation laws.

During the next 55 years, there were many attempts to give blacks the same rights as whites and some progress was made. It wasn't until Martin Luther King challenged the bus segregation laws in Montgomery that change really started to happen.

At last, in 1964 the Civil Rights Act, which banned discrimination, was passed by Congress. This was followed the next year by the Voting Rights Act. In a speech to Congress, Lyndon B Johnson, said that the act would 'allow men and women to register and vote, whatever the colour of their skin.'

Timeline

1929 15 Jan   Martin Luther King born in
Atlanta, Georgia (USA).

1954   Martin becomes a church
minister in Montgomery,
Alabama.

1955 Dec   Rosa Parks arrested for taking
a white bus seat. Martin leads
the Montgomery bus boycott.

1956 21 Feb   Martin jailed for the first time.

13 Nov   Supreme Court rules that bus
segregation is illegal. Many
states ignored the ruling.

21 Dec   Montgomery buses desegregated.
Sit-ins begin all over the south.

1963 2 May   A thousand black children
march through Birmingham.

28 Aug   Martin gives 'I Have A Dream'
speech in Washington.

1964 10 Dec   Martin is the youngest person
to receive the Nobel Peace Prize.

1968 4 April   Martin shot dead in Memphis,
Tennessee.

More information

Books to read

Let the Trumpet Sound. A Life of Martin Luther King by Stephen B Oates, Canongate 1998.
Martin Luther King, Jr by Peter and Connie Roop, Heinemann 1998.
Martin Luther King by Valerie Schloredt and Pam Brown, Exley Publications 1988.
I Have a Dream. The Story of Martin Luther King by Neil Tonge, Hodder Wayland 2000.

Websites
http://martinlutherking.8m.com/
http://www.seattletimes.com/mlk/

Museum
The National Civil Rights Museum is in Memphis, Tennessee, USA on the site of Martin Luther King's assassination. Their website includes a virtual tour of the museum:
http://www.midsouth.rr.com /civilrights

Glossary

assassination The killing of a well-known person.

boycott Refusing to use or buy something from someone else.

civil rights A person's right to be free and equal with others.

governor The person in charge of a US state.

justice When all is right and fair.

Ku Klux Klan A white secret society dedicated to keeping segregation.

Lincoln, Abraham US President 1861-5, ended slavery after winning the Civil War; assassinated by a racist.

nigger An insulting name for a black person.

racist Someone who believes that one race is better than another.

segregation Keeping people apart.

slave A person owned by another.

Supreme Court The highest court in the USA.

Index